W9-BNC-529

WITHDRAWN

WELCOME TO MY COUNTRY

Welcome to
ISRAEL

Gareth Stevens Publishing
A WORLD ALMANAC EDUCATION GROUP COMPANY

Written by
GERALDINE MESENAS/FREDERICK FISHER

Designed by
HASNAH MOHD ESA

Picture research by
SUSAN JANE MANUEL

First published in North America in 2001 by
Gareth Stevens Publishing
A World Almanac Education Group Company
330 West Olive Street, Suite 100
Milwaukee, Wisconsin 53212 USA

For a free color catalog describing
Gareth Stevens' list of high-quality books
and multimedia programs, call
1-800-542-2595 (USA) or
1-800-461-9120 (CANADA).
Gareth Stevens Publishing's
Fax: (414) 332-3567.

© **TIMES EDITIONS PTE LTD 2001**
Originated and designed by
Times Editions
An imprint of Times Media Private Limited
A member of the Times Publishing Group
Times Centre, 1 New Industrial Road
Singapore 536196
http://www.timesone.com.sg/te

Library of Congress Cataloging-in-Publication Data
Mesenas, Geraldine.
Welcome to Israel / Geraldine Mesenas and Frederick Fisher.
p. cm. -- (Welcome to my country)
Includes bibliographical references and index.
ISBN 0-8368-2519-5 (lib. bdg.)
1. Israel--Juvenile literature. 2. Israel--Pictorial works. [1. Israel.]
I. Fisher, Frederick. II. Title. III. Series.
DS118 .M588   2001
956.9405--dc21   00-057351

Printed in Malaysia

1 2 3 4 5 6 7 8 9 05 04 03 02 01

Contents

Words that appear in the glossary are printed in **boldface** type the first time they occur in the text.

Welcome to Israel!

Situated in the Middle East, Israel is diverse in geography, **ethnicity**, and religion. Israel became independent in 1948. Today, **immigrants** from all over the world settle there and contribute to its incredible culture. Let's learn about Israel, its people, and its remarkable history.

Opposite: The capital of Israel is Jerusalem. It is one of the oldest cities in the world.

Below: During Sukkot, a festival of thanksgiving, people sell citron and willow on the streets.

The Flag of Israel

The Israeli national flag features two blue stripes at the top and bottom and the Magen David (Shield of David) on a white background. The Magen David has been an official symbol of Jewish people since the 1600s.

The Land

Israel has an area of 7,992 square miles (20,700 square kilometers). The Israeli and Palestinian governments are now arguing over the ownership of East Jerusalem, the Gaza Strip, the West Bank, and the Golan Heights.

The Mediterranean Sea lies to the west of Israel, Lebanon to the north, Syria to the northeast, Jordan to the east, and Egypt to the southwest. Most Israeli cities are located on the plains along the Mediterranean's west coast.

Below: The Sea of Galilee in northeastern Israel is home to many nature reserves.

Deserts and Rivers

The Negev stretches across the southern region of Israel. It covers about half of the country and is home to Arab **nomads** and other people. To the north, the Judean Desert separates Jerusalem from the Dead Sea, which is so salty that no animal or plant life can survive in it. The major river in Israel is the Jordan River, which starts at Mount Hermon in Syria and empties into the Dead Sea. The waters of the Jordan River **irrigate** crops for farmers in Israel and Jordan.

Climate

Israel has a subtropical climate. The western coast is the coolest region, with temperatures that range from about 65° to 90° Fahrenheit (18° to 32° Celsius). The hottest region is the Arava Valley, where temperatures go as high as 114° F (46° C) and the annual rainfall can be as little as 1 inch (2.5 centimeters). The rainy season lasts from November to April. Averaging 44 inches (112 cm), Northern Galilee receives the most rain.

Above:
Beaches along the Mediterranean coast are a favorite destination for Israelis during the summer season.

Opposite: A lovely cactus garden in En Gedi overlooks the Dead Sea.

Plants and Animals

Israel is home to over 2,800 species of plants, such as honeysuckle, pistachio and eucalyptus trees, and many types of flowers, including irises and tulips.

Many species of birds, reptiles, and mammals are also found in Israel, including wolves, gazelles, wildcats, and hares. Over 150 nature reserves in Israel provide protection for many endangered plant and animal species.

Above: The ibex, a mountain goat, lives in the Hai Bar Reserve.

History

In 1125 B.C., the Hebrews defeated the Egyptians in Palestine (also called the *Holy Land* or *Canaan*) and became known as the Israelites. In 990 B.C., King David made Jerusalem his capital. When David's son, King Solomon, died, the kingdom was divided into Israel and Judah. The Babylonians conquered Jerusalem in 586 B.C. and forced many Israelites into exile for fifty years.

Below: In 37 B.C., the Romans appointed Herod the Great to be king of Judah. During his reign, he built **the aqueducts** of Caesarea.

Left: In A.D. 636, Muslim Arabs invaded Palestine and made Jerusalem a base for Islam. In 1095, European leaders launched military campaigns, called the Crusades, to take over Jerusalem in the name of Christianity.

Over the next thousand years, the Persians, Greeks, Turks, and Romans invaded Palestine, so sometimes the area was Muslim, and other times, it was Christian. In A.D. 66, the Roman Empire violently attacked Jews who revolted against Roman rule. From A.D. 636 to the 1200s, Palestine was controlled by Muslim Arabs, then Egyptians, then Mongols from China. The Ottoman Turks, who were Muslim, ruled Palestine from 1517 to 1917.

Below: Greek leader Alexander the Great conquered Palestine in 333 B.C.

Zionism

Over the centuries, many Jews settled in Europe and North America, where they faced **anti-Semitic persecution**. The late 1800s saw the rise of **Zionism**, a nationalist movement among Jews who wanted to immigrate to Israel. Theodor Herzl tried to create an independent Jewish settlement in Palestine, but the Ottoman Turkish government rejected his plan. In 1914, only about 90,000 Jewish people lived in Palestine.

Above: Austrian journalist Theodor Herzl organized the first Zionist Congress in Switzerland in 1897.

The World Wars and the Holocaust

During World War I, Britain wanted world Jewish support in the fight against Germany, so Britain supported creating a Jewish state. By 1922, Britain governed Palestine. By 1933, over 238,000 Jews lived in Palestine.

In Europe, during World War II, over six million Jews were killed in the **Holocaust**. The war ended in 1945, and many surviving European Jews moved to Palestine. On May 14, 1948, David Ben-Gurion, head of the Zionist Executive, declared the establishment of a new Jewish state in Palestine.

Above: Between 1940 and 1945, over six million Jews died in Nazi **concentration camps** in Europe. Prisoners were forced to wear badges in the shape of the Magen David.

Twentieth-Century Conflicts

From 1948 to the 1970s, Israel was at war in the Middle East with Arabs who had been living in Palestine and who refused to accept the new State of Israel. Israel and Arab countries signed a major peace **accord** in 1979. However, conflicts continued between Israel and the Palestine Liberation Organization (PLO), which has used **terrorism** in trying to create a separate Palestinian state. Today, negotiations continue over self-rule for Palestinians in the Gaza Strip and West Bank.

David Ben-Gurion (1886–1973)

David Ben-Gurion declared Israel's independence on May 14, 1948. He was Israel's first prime minister, serving from 1948 to 1953 and again from 1955 to 1963.

David Ben-Gurion

Golda Meir (1898–1978)

Golda Meir was one of the founders of the State of Israel. She became the first female prime minister of Israel in 1969 and resigned in 1974.

Golda Meir

Yitzhak Rabin (1922–1995)

Yitzhak Rabin became Israel's prime minister in 1974 and again in 1992. Rabin tried to secure peace between Israel and its neighbors. In 1994, Rabin, Israeli foreign minister Shimon Peres, and Yasir Arafat received the Nobel Prize for Peace. Rabin was **assassinated** in 1995.

Yitzhak Rabin

Government and the Economy

Israel is a **parliamentary republic**. The legislative body, or Knesset, consists of 120 members who are elected to a four-year term. The Knesset makes laws and deals with social and defense issues. The Knesset also elects the president, who is the head of state.

Below: The Knesset writes laws and debates issues on immigration, defense, social welfare, and the status of women.

The prime minister and the cabinet of ministers are responsible for both the internal and foreign affairs of the country.

Israeli citizens aged eighteen and above can vote. The people elect a prime minister and a parliamentary party. No single political party controls the Knesset. The two major political parties are the Labor Party, a social democratic party, and the Likud party, a conservative party that was established in 1973.

Above: Ehud Barak (*left*) of the Labor Party became prime minister in 1999. He won the 1999 election against Likud party leader Benjamin Netanyahu (*right*), who, in 1996, was the first Israeli prime minister to be elected by popular vote.

Economy

Ten percent of Israel's income is spent on national defense. The country is also trying to build a modern **infrastructure** and provide the best roads, bridges, schools, and public services possible for its people.

Although the Israeli economy has grown rapidly, the country has huge debts. Israel imports more goods than it exports, so the government depends on foreign loans and aid.

Above: The seaport of Tel Aviv-Yafo is one of Israel's most important ports.

Major industries in Israel include chemicals, cut diamonds, textiles, telecommunications, and high-tech products, such as computers.

Two types of farming settlements are special to Israel. In a kibbutz, people split the work and the profits equally. In a *moshav* (moh-SHAHV), farmers work individually but put what they grow into shared storage.

Below: Palestinian farm workers harvest chilies in the Gaza Strip.

People and Lifestyle

Israel's population is 5.8 million, of which 81 percent are Jews. Jews from all over the world have been steadily immigrating to Israel since the late 1800s. More than half of Israel's Jewish population are Israeli-born Jews, or *sabras* (ZAH-braz). The main Jewish

Left: A strict form of Judaism is Hasidism, which has detailed rules concerning marriage, food, and other aspects of life. Hasidic Jews wear traditional, black clothing, and the men have curly locks down each side of the face.

groups in Israel are the Ashkenazim, whose origins are from Central and Eastern Europe, and the Sephardim, whose origins are from Spain, North Africa, and the Middle East.

The two largest groups of the non-Jewish population are Muslim Arabs and Christian Arabs. Muslim Arabs often live in rural areas. Christian Arabs live in the cities. Other minority groups include the Circassians, the Baha'is, the Samaritans, and the Druze, who accept no new members.

Family Life

Religion affects all aspects of Israeli family life. Most Israeli Jews are non-Orthodox Jews. Their religious practices are more modern than those of Orthodox Jews, and many have Western-oriented family lifestyles. Orthodox Jews observe strict, traditional ways and tend to have very large families. Orthodox Jews make sure their children follow the Jewish religion closely.

Rural and Urban Life

Over 90 percent of Israelis live in urban areas. About 25 percent live in the cities of Jerusalem, Tel Aviv-Yafo, and Haifa.

Rural settlements in Israel include the kibbutz, in which several families live and work together, and the moshav, which is becoming more popular as it gives families more independence.

Left: A street musician in Jerusalem rests between songs.

Education

In 1949, the Israeli government passed the Compulsory Education Law. Under this law, children between the ages of five and eighteen receive **compulsory**, free schooling. At the age of five, Israeli children go to kindergarten for a year, followed by six years of primary education. Junior high school begins at the age of twelve and lasts three years. High school also lasts three years.

Above: A student presents her project at the Yonatan Elementary School in Netanya.

24

Jewish children attend classes in Hebrew. Christian and Muslim Arabs, as well as Druze, are taught in Arabic.

After high school, students can continue their studies at a university, trade school, or other institution of higher learning. Major universities include the Hebrew University of Jerusalem and Tel Aviv University.

Left: Israeli students wave Israeli national flags during a student rally in Jerusalem.

Religion

Israel does not have an official state religion. The main religions in Israel are Judaism, Islam, Christianity, Druze, and Bahaism.

Judaism was founded by Abraham in about 2000 B.C. Its practices and traditions are based on the Torah (the first five books of the Bible) and the Talmud (a scholarly text written by Jewish scholars on the Mishna). The Mishna is a code of oral laws first written down in A.D. 200.

Above: Hasidism is a form of Orthodox Judaism. Hasidic Jews make up a small community in Israel.

Opposite: The Church of the Holy Sepulcher in Jerusalem is built where Jesus Christ was buried after he was **crucified.** Galilee and Jerusalem are two of the most sacred places in the Christian world.

The Muslim community includes Arabs and Circassians. Jerusalem was a Muslim stronghold for many centuries before the Israelis made it the capital of their new homeland in 1948. Christians in Israel are mostly Greek Catholic, Greek Orthodox, or Roman Catholic. The Druze practice a secret religion, which forbids intermarriage and changing one's religion. The Baha'i faith, founded in Iran in 1844, says that all world religions share one message.

Above: Located in Jerusalem, the beautiful Dome of the Rock is a holy Muslim shrine.

Language

Hebrew and Arabic are the official languages of Israel. Hebrew is the most widely used language in Israel.

In the past, Jews used Hebrew only in prayer and study. The arrival of many immigrants made a common language

Left: Israelis, like this man in Old Jerusalem, read about current events in newspapers.

necessary, so Hebrew was revived. In 1890, Eliezer Ben-Yehuda started the Hebrew Language Council, which wrote a dictionary and encouraged the use of Hebrew in schools and books.

The most important writers in Israel include novelist Schmuel Yosef Agnon (1888–1970), who won the Nobel Prize for Literature in 1966, and poet Haim Nahman Bialik (1873–1934). Famous modern Israeli writers include A. B. Yehoshua and Amos Oz.

Below: A. B. Yehoshua was born in Jerusalem in 1936. He has written a wide selection of novels, essays, and plays. He received the Israel Prize for Literature in 1995.

Arts

Bulgarian-born Boris Schatz established the Bezalel Academy of Arts and Crafts in 1906. Bezalel aimed to create an "original Jewish art," combining European and Middle Eastern elements. By the 1920s, newer immigrant artists rejected Bezalel's style and started

Left: This sculpture at Jerusalem's Yad Vashem Museum symbolizes the tragic suffering of Jews in Nazi concentration camps during the Holocaust of World War II.

looking for their own cultural identity. Many artists then favored the young city of Tel Aviv, founded in 1909. Today, Tel Aviv continues to be Israel's center for the arts.

Music

Classical music is well-established in Israel. The Israel Philharmonic Orchestra performs with world-famous conductors and musicians every year. Famous Israeli musicians include Itzhak Perlman and Pinchas Zukerman. Over two hundred music conservatories, or schools, exist in Israel.

Left: A klezmer band entertains at a Jewish folk music festival.

Folk music also thrives in Israel. One of the most popular forms of folk music among the Jews is klezmer, which came from Eastern European Jewish culture and features an expressive clarinet.

Performing Arts and Cinema

Israel's national theater, Habimah, is located in Tel Aviv. Both traditional and modern Hebrew works are performed at Habimah.

Folk dancing in Israel has been influenced by the Eastern Europeans, Arabs, and North Africans. Israelis also enjoy modern dance and classical ballet.

Israeli cinema began in the 1950s, and Israeli movies have many themes, from the Holocaust to everyday life in

Above: Jewish folk dancers perform a lively dance.

modern-day Israel. The Israel Film Center provides funds for local production companies and promotes Israeli films overseas.

Museums

Museums in Israel house contemporary art, religious art, ethnic art, and **archaeological** finds. They also have exhibits on history and architecture. The Tel Aviv Museum of Art has some of the best art collections in Israel.

Below: The Tel Aviv Museum of Art attracts crowds of visitors every year.

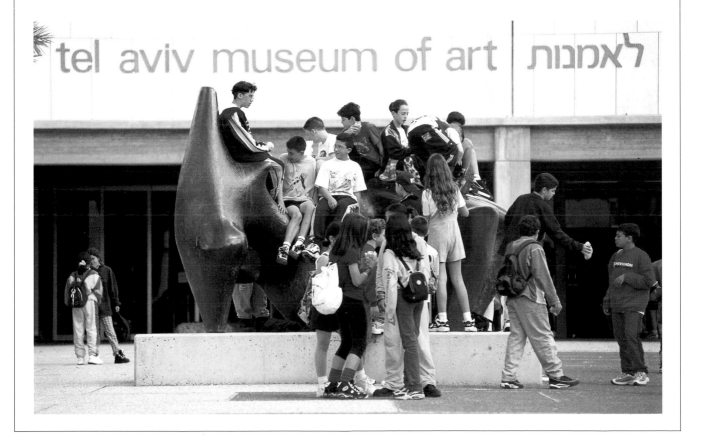

Leisure

Israeli Jews take only one day off every week on the *Shabbat* (shah-BAHT), or Sabbath. Israelis living in the cities enjoy shopping, playing sports, nightclubbing, going to movies and concerts, or meeting up with friends to chat in cafés. The beaches along the Mediterranean coast and at the resorts in Eilat are also popular destinations. Israelis in rural areas often spend their leisure time with their families.

Below: City-dwellers enjoy meeting friends at restaurants and cafés for a meal and a chat.

Israelis love to read. They read more books than any other people in the world. Over a thousand libraries exist in Israel, and book fairs and bookstores are popular. In Israel, a wide variety of magazines, newspapers, and books is printed in many languages.

Sports

Popular sports in Israel include soccer, basketball, tennis, volleyball, and water sports such as swimming, sailing, diving, snorkeling, and windsurfing. In soccer, basketball, and volleyball, Israel's national teams compete in European leagues.

In 1932, the first Maccabiah Games, or the Jewish Olympics, were held in Palestine. The games were halted in

Above:
Windsurfers are a common sight off the coast of Tel Aviv-Yafo.

1935 because of the Nazi movement in Germany, but the Maccabiah Games resumed in 1950 after World War II. Jewish athletes from all over the world participate in the games. Events include swimming, soccer, track and field, wrestling, karate, and volleyball.

Israel's national judo team gave Israel its first Olympic medals in the 1992 Olympic Games in Barcelona, Spain. Israel has competed in the Olympic Games since 1952.

Left: Young boys learn martial arts at a youth club.

Festivals

The Jewish New Year, called Rosh Hashanah, is celebrated on the first and second days of *Tishri* (TISH-ree), the first month of the Jewish calendar. On the tenth day of Tishri, Jews celebrate Yom Kippur, when they fast and pray for forgiveness for their sins.

Hanukkah starts on the twenty-fifth day of *Kislev* (KEYS-lev), the third Jewish month. This celebration lasts for eight days. During Hanukkah, Jews pray, play games, and exchange gifts.

Above: When a Jewish boy turns thirteen, a *bar mitzvah* (bar MITTS-vah) ceremony is carried out to celebrate his entry into the adult Jewish community. A similar ceremony for girls is called a *bat mitzvah* (baht MITTS-vah).

Opposite: During Hanukkah, Israelis light the **menorah**.

Passover begins on the fourteenth day of *Nisan* (NEE-san), the seventh month in the Jewish calendar. Lasting seven days, Passover celebrates the **liberation** of the Jews from slavery.

Muslim holidays include Ramadan and Eid al-Adha. Christians celebrate Christmas and Easter. Other important holidays include Independence Day and Holocaust Memorial Day.

Above: Held in spring, Purim is a happy holiday filled with carnivals and fun.

Food

Israeli cooking has been influenced by traditional Jewish, Eastern European, Middle Eastern, and North African foods. Favorite Jewish foods include gefilte fish, or fish balls, and *kishkes* (KISH-keys), or sausages. Two types of Jewish bread popular in Israel and other parts of the world are doughnut-shaped bagels and slightly sweet, braided *challah* (KHAH-lah).

Below: Bagels are popular among the Israelis.

Left: People living along the coast eat fresh fish every day.

Immigrants from all over the world have brought their foods to Israel as well. Eastern Europeans enjoy *cholent* (KHO-lent), a stew made with meat and potato, and *latkes* (LAHT-keys), or fried potato pancakes. Arabs from the Middle East enjoy spicy food.

Both Jews and Muslims follow strict dietary laws. They cannot eat certain foods or use certain methods of food preparation. For Jews, only meat from animals killed a certain way is considered kosher, or proper. Pork and shellfish are never allowed.

Below: A Druze woman serves a plate of fresh bread.

ISRAEL

LEBANON

SYRIA

Mount Hermon
(9,232 ft/2,814 m) ▲

Mount Meron
(3,964 ft/1,208 m) ▲

GOLAN
HEIGHTS

G A L I L E E

● Karmiel

Sea of
Galilee

Haifa ●

● Nazareth

MEDITERRANEAN

SEA

Caesarea ⋰

WEST
BANK

Jordan

Netanya ●

Tel Aviv-Yafo ●
Bat Yam ●●
Holon ●

JERUSALEM ■

● Kaliya

Judean Desert

Dead
Sea

GAZA
STRIP

J U D E A

● En Gedi

Beersheba ●

N E G E V

Arava Valley

EGYPT

JORDAN

▬▬▬	State Boundary
──	Provincial Boundary
─ ─ ─	Equator
■	Capital
●	City
⋰	Historical Site
～	River

N
↑

● Eilat

Above: Haifa, in northwestern Israel, has many beaches along the Mediterranean Sea.

Arava Valley C4–C5

Bat Yam B2
Beersheba B3

Caesarea B2

Dead Sea C3

Egypt A3–B5
Eilat B5
En Gedi C3

Galilee C1
Gaza Strip B3
Golan Heights C1

Haifa B1
Holon B2

Jerusalem C3
Jordan C2–D5
Jordan River C1–C3
Judea B3–C3
Judean Desert C3

Kaliya C3
Karmiel C1

Lebanon C1

Mediterranean Sea
  A1–B3

Mount Hermon C1
Mount Meron C1

Nazareth C2
Negev B3–C4
Netanya B2

Sea of Galilee
  C1–C2
Syria D1

Tel Aviv-Yafo B2

West Bank C2–C3

Quick Facts

Official Name   Medinat Yisra'el, State of Israel

Capital   Jerusalem

Official Languages   Hebrew, Arabic

Population   5,749,760 (July 1999 estimate)

Land Area   7,992 square miles (20,700 square kilometers)

Highest Point   Mount Meron 3,964 feet (1,208 meters)

Major River   Jordan

Lakes and Seas   Dead Sea, Sea of Galilee (Lake Kinneret)

Major Cities   Bat Yam, Beersheba, Haifa, Holon, Jerusalem, Tel Aviv-Yafo

Major Religions   Judaism, Islam, Christianity, Bahaism, Druze

Religious Holidays   Christmas, Easter, Good Friday (Christian); Hanukkah, Passover, Purim, Rosh Hashanah, Sukkot, Yom Kippur, (Jewish); Eid al-Adha, Eid al-Fitr, Ramadan (Muslim)

Secular Holidays   Holocaust Memorial Day, Independence Day, Memorial Day

Currency   New Israeli shekel (4.135 NIS = U.S. $1 in 2000)

Opposite: Built in the sixth century, the St. George Monastery is located near Jerusalem.

Glossary

accord: agreement.

anti-Semitic: hostile toward or prejudiced against Jews.

aqueducts: man-made canals that carry water over a distance.

archaeological: having to do with early civilizations and the analysis of ancient objects.

assassinated: killed for political reasons.

bar mitzvah (bar MITTS-vah)**:** a ceremony marking a 13-year-old Jewish boy's entry into adulthood.

bat mitzvah (baht MITTS-vah)**:** a ceremony marking a 13-year-old Jewish girl's entry into adulthood.

challah (KHAH-lah)**:** a braided white bread made with eggs and honey.

compulsory: required; must be done.

concentration camps: military camps used to collect, imprison, and persecute certain people.

crucified: put to death by nailing or tying the hands and feet to a cross.

ethnicity: membership in one race or cultural group.

Holocaust: the mass killing of European Jews in Nazi concentration camps during World War II.

immigrants: people who move into a new country from a different country.

infrastructure: bridges, roads, and other basic facilities serving a country.

irrigate: to bring water to farm crops by using ditches or pipes.

kibbutz (key-BOOTS)**:** a rural Israeli settlement in which members share all economic responsibilities.

kishkes (KISH-keys)**:** sausages made of flour, chicken fat, meat, and onions.

liberation: the act of being set free.

menorah: a candle holder with seven or nine candles, used for Jewish religious services and festivals.

moshav (moh-SHAHV)**:** a village where independent farmers share the harvests.

nomads: people who move from place to place and often live in tents.

parliamentary republic: a type of government with an elected cabinet of ministers headed by a prime minister or president.

persecution: constant injury or harm because of a person's culture.

Shabbat (shah-BAHT)**:** the Sabbath day; the seventh day of the week.

terrorism: the use of violence to achieve political goals.

Zionism: an international Jewish movement that was founded to establish a Jewish state in Palestine.

More Books to Read

The Gang of Four: Nest of the Jerusalem Eagle. Yaacov Peterseil (Pitspopany Press)

Israel. Country Fact Files series. Jose Patterson (Raintree/Steck-Vaughn)

Israel. Festivals of the World series. Don Foy (Gareth Stevens)

Israel: The Culture. Lands, Peoples, and Cultures series. Debbie Smith (Crabtree Publishing)

Israel: The Founding of a Modern Nation. Maida Silverman (Dial Books for Young Readers)

Jerusalem and the Holy Land: Chronicles from National Geographic. Arthur M. Schlesinger and Fred L. Israel (Chelsea House)

Letters Home from Israel. Letters Home From series. Marcia S. Gresko (Blackbirch Marketing)

Life on an Israeli Kibbutz. The Way People Live series. Linda Jacobs Altman (Lucent Books)

The Middle East in Search of Peace. Headliners series. Cathryn J. Long (Millbrook Press)

Videos

Amazing Wonders of the World: From Egypt to Israel. (Questar)

Israel: A Land for Everyone. (IVN Entertainment)

This is Israel. (Sisu Home Entertainment)

Touring Israel: The Nation for the Next Millennium. (Questar)

Web Sites

www.akhlah.com/

www.israel-mfa.gov.il/mfa/israel50/ posters.html

jeru.huji.ac.il/open_screen2.htm

Due to the dynamic nature of the Internet, some web sites stay current longer than others. To find additional web sites, use a reliable search engine with one or more of the following keywords to help you locate information about Israel. Keywords: *Bethlehem, Galilee, Hebrew, Holocaust, Jerusalem, Jews, kibbutz, Palestine.*

Index